THE ONE-YEAR
PRAYER
jOURNAL
A GiRL'S NOTEBOOK

WRiTTEN & DESiGNED BY SHALANA FRiSBY

Don't forget to grab your bonus freebies today!

WWW.123JOURNALIT.COM / FREEBIES
SCRIPTURE FLASHCARDS - BIBLE READING PROMPTS - JOURNALING PAGES

More information at: www.123journalit.com

First Printing: May 2018
1 2 3 Journal It Publishing

ISBN-13: 978-1-947209-57-2
Pocketbook 6x9-in. Format Size
From the *Christian Workbooks* Series

THiS jOURNAL
BELONGS TO

_____

MY PRAYER NOTES FOR THE WEEK OF _____ TO _____

MONDAY:

TUESDAY:

WEDNESDAY:

THURSDAY:

FRIDAY:

SATURDAY:

SUNDAY:

ANSWERED PRAYERS & THiNGS i'M THANKFUL FOR THiS WEEK:

_____

_____

_____

_____

_____

_____

MY PRAYER NOTES FOR THE WEEK OF _____ TO _____

MONDAY:

TUESDAY:

WEDNESDAY:

THURSDAY:

FRiDAY:

SATURDAY:

SUNDAY:

ANSWERED PRAYERS & THiNGS i'M THANKFUL FOR THiS WEEK:

MY PRAYER NOTES FOR THE WEEK OF _____ TO _____

MONDAY:

TUESDAY:

WEDNESDAY:

THURSDAY:

FRIDAY:

- -
- -
- -
- -

SATURDAY:

- -
- -
- -
- -

SUNDAY:

- -
- -
- -
- -

ANSWERED PRAYERS & THINGS I'M THANKFUL FOR THIS WEEK:

MY PRAYER NOTES FOR THE WEEK OF _____ TO _____

MONDAY:

TUESDAY:

WEDNESDAY:

THURSDAY:

FRIDAY:

SATURDAY:

SUNDAY:

ANSWERED PRAYERS & THINGS I'M THANKFUL FOR THIS WEEK:

_____

_____

_____

_____

_____

MY PRAYER NOTES FOR THE WEEK OF _____ TO _____

MONDAY:

TUESDAY:

WEDNESDAY:

THURSDAY:

FRiDAY:

SATURDAY:

SUNDAY:

ANSWERED PRAYERS & THiNGS i'M THANKFUL FOR THiS WEEK:

MY PRAYER NOTES FOR THE WEEK OF _____ TO _____

MONDAY:

TUESDAY:

WEDNESDAY:

THURSDAY:

FRIDAY:

SATURDAY:

SUNDAY:

ANSWERED PRAYERS & THINGS I'M THANKFUL FOR THIS WEEK:

MY PRAYER NOTES FOR THE WEEK OF _____ TO _____

MONDAY:

TUESDAY:

WEDNESDAY:

THURSDAY:

FRIDAY:

SATURDAY:

SUNDAY:

ANSWERED PRAYERS & THINGS I'M THANKFUL FOR THIS WEEK:

MY PRAYER NOTES FOR THE WEEK OF _____ TO _____

MONDAY:

TUESDAY:

WEDNESDAY:

THURSDAY:

FRIDAY:

SATURDAY:

SUNDAY:

ANSWERED PRAYERS & THINGS I'M THANKFUL FOR THIS WEEK:

MY PRAYER NOTES FOR THE WEEK OF _____ TO _____

MONDAY:

TUESDAY:

WEDNESDAY:

THURSDAY:

FRIDAY:

SATURDAY:

SUNDAY:

ANSWERED PRAYERS & THINGS I'M THANKFUL FOR THIS WEEK:

_____

_____

_____

_____

_____

MY PRAYER NOTES FOR THE WEEK OF _____ TO _____

MONDAY:

TUESDAY:

WEDNESDAY:

THURSDAY:

FRIDAY:

SATURDAY:

SUNDAY:

ANSWERED PRAYERS & THINGS I'M THANKFUL FOR THIS WEEK:

MY PRAYER NOTES FOR THE WEEK OF _____ TO _____

MONDAY:

TUESDAY:

WEDNESDAY:

THURSDAY:

FRIDAY:

SATURDAY:

SUNDAY:

ANSWERED PRAYERS & THINGS I'M THANKFUL FOR THIS WEEK:

MY PRAYER NOTES FOR THE WEEK OF _____ TO _____

MONDAY:

TUESDAY:

WEDNESDAY:

THURSDAY:

FRiDAY:

- -
- -
- -
- -

SATURDAY:

- -
- -
- -
- -

SUNDAY:

- -
- -
- -
- -

ANSWERED PRAYERS & THiNGS i'M THANKFUL FOR THiS WEEK:

_____

_____

_____

_____

_____

MY PRAYER NOTES FOR THE WEEK OF _____ TO _____

MONDAY:

TUESDAY:

WEDNESDAY:

THURSDAY:

FRIDAY:

SATURDAY:

SUNDAY:

ANSWERED PRAYERS & THINGS I'M THANKFUL FOR THIS WEEK:

_____

_____

_____

_____

_____

_____

MY PRAYER NOTES FOR THE WEEK OF _____ TO _____

MONDAY:

_____

_____

_____

_____

TUESDAY:

_____

_____

_____

_____

WEDNESDAY:

_____

_____

_____

_____

THURSDAY:

_____

_____

_____

_____

FRIDAY:

SATURDAY:

SUNDAY:

ANSWERED PRAYERS & THINGS I'M THANKFUL FOR THIS WEEK:

_____
_____
_____
_____
_____
_____

MY PRAYER NOTES FOR THE WEEK OF _____ TO _____

MONDAY:

TUESDAY:

WEDNESDAY:

THURSDAY:

FRIDAY:

SATURDAY:

SUNDAY:

ANSWERED PRAYERS & THINGS I'M THANKFUL FOR THIS WEEK:

_____
_____
_____
_____
_____

MY PRAYER NOTES FOR THE WEEK OF _____ TO _____

MONDAY:

TUESDAY:

WEDNESDAY:

THURSDAY:

FRIDAY:

SATURDAY:

SUNDAY:

ANSWERED PRAYERS & THINGS I'M THANKFUL FOR THIS WEEK:

_____

_____

_____

_____

_____

_____

MY PRAYER NOTES FOR THE WEEK OF _____ TO _____

MONDAY:

_____

_____

_____

_____

TUESDAY:

_____

_____

_____

_____

WEDNESDAY:

_____

_____

_____

_____

THURSDAY:

_____

_____

_____

_____

FRIDAY:

_____

_____

_____

_____

SATURDAY:

_____

_____

_____

_____

SUNDAY:

_____

_____

_____

_____

ANSWERED PRAYERS & THINGS I'M THANKFUL FOR THIS WEEK:

_____

_____

_____

_____

_____

_____

MY PRAYER NOTES FOR THE WEEK OF _____ TO _____

MONDAY:

TUESDAY:

WEDNESDAY:

THURSDAY:

FRIDAY:

SATURDAY:

SUNDAY:

ANSWERED PRAYERS & THINGS I'M THANKFUL FOR THIS WEEK:

MY PRAYER NOTES FOR THE WEEK OF _____ TO _____

MONDAY:

TUESDAY:

WEDNESDAY:

THURSDAY:

FRIDAY:

- -
- -
- -
- -

SATURDAY:

- -
- -
- -
- -

SUNDAY:

- -
- -
- -
- -

ANSWERED PRAYERS & THINGS I'M THANKFUL FOR THIS WEEK:

_____

_____

_____

_____

_____

_____

MY PRAYER NOTES FOR THE WEEK OF _____ TO _____

MONDAY:

TUESDAY:

WEDNESDAY:

THURSDAY:

FRIDAY:

SATURDAY:

SUNDAY:

ANSWERED PRAYERS & THINGS I'M THANKFUL FOR THIS WEEK:

_____

_____

_____

_____

_____

_____

MY PRAYER NOTES FOR THE WEEK OF _____ TO _____

MONDAY:

TUESDAY:

WEDNESDAY:

THURSDAY:

FRIDAY:

- -
- -
- -
- -

SATURDAY:

- -
- -
- -
- -

SUNDAY:

- -
- -
- -
- -

ANSWERED PRAYERS & THINGS I'M THANKFUL FOR THIS WEEK:

_____

_____

_____

_____

_____

MY PRAYER NOTES FOR THE WEEK OF _____ TO _____

MONDAY:

TUESDAY:

WEDNESDAY:

THURSDAY:

FRIDAY:

SATURDAY:

SUNDAY:

ANSWERED PRAYERS & THINGS I'M THANKFUL FOR THIS WEEK:

MY PRAYER NOTES FOR THE WEEK OF _____ TO _____

MONDAY:

TUESDAY:

WEDNESDAY:

THURSDAY:

FRiDAY:

SATURDAY:

SUNDAY:

ANSWERED PRAYERS & THiNGS i'M THANKFUL FOR THiS WEEK:

MY PRAYER NOTES FOR THE WEEK OF _____ TO _____

MONDAY:

TUESDAY:

WEDNESDAY:

THURSDAY:

FRiDAY:

SATURDAY:

SUNDAY:

ANSWERED PRAYERS & THiNGS i'M THANKFUL FOR THiS WEEK:

_____
_____
_____
_____
_____

MY PRAYER NOTES FOR THE WEEK OF _____ TO _____

MONDAY:

TUESDAY:

WEDNESDAY:

THURSDAY:

FRIDAY:

- -
- -
- -
- -

SATURDAY:

- -
- -
- -
- -

SUNDAY:

- -
- -
- -
- -

ANSWERED PRAYERS & THINGS I'M THANKFUL FOR THIS WEEK:

_____

_____

_____

_____

_____

_____

MY PRAYER NOTES FOR THE WEEK OF _____ TO _____

MONDAY:
_____
_____
_____
_____

TUESDAY:
_____
_____
_____
_____

WEDNESDAY:
_____
_____
_____
_____

THURSDAY:
_____
_____
_____
_____

FRIDAY:

_____
_____
_____
_____

SATURDAY:

_____
_____
_____
_____

SUNDAY:

_____
_____
_____
_____

ANSWERED PRAYERS & THINGS I'M THANKFUL FOR THIS WEEK:

_____
_____
_____
_____
_____
_____

MY PRAYER NOTES FOR THE WEEK OF _____ TO _____

MONDAY:

TUESDAY:

WEDNESDAY:

THURSDAY:

FRIDAY:

SATURDAY:

SUNDAY:

ANSWERED PRAYERS & THINGS I'M THANKFUL FOR THIS WEEK:

MY PRAYER NOTES FOR THE WEEK OF _____ TO _____

MONDAY:

TUESDAY:

WEDNESDAY:

THURSDAY:

FRIDAY:

SATURDAY:

SUNDAY:

ANSWERED PRAYERS & THINGS I'M THANKFUL FOR THIS WEEK:

_____

_____

_____

_____

_____

_____

MY PRAYER NOTES FOR THE WEEK OF _____ TO _____

MONDAY:

TUESDAY:

WEDNESDAY:

THURSDAY:

FRIDAY:

- -
- -
- -
- -

SATURDAY:

- -
- -
- -
- -

SUNDAY:

- -
- -
- -
- -

ANSWERED PRAYERS & THINGS I'M THANKFUL FOR THIS WEEK:

MY PRAYER NOTES FOR THE WEEK OF _____ TO _____

MONDAY:

TUESDAY:

WEDNESDAY:

THURSDAY:

FRIDAY:

_____

_____

_____

_____

SATURDAY:

_____

_____

_____

_____

SUNDAY:

_____

_____

_____

_____

ANSWERED PRAYERS & THINGS I'M THANKFUL FOR THIS WEEK:

_____

_____

_____

_____

_____

_____

MY PRAYER NOTES FOR THE WEEK OF _____ TO _____

MONDAY:

TUESDAY:

WEDNESDAY:

THURSDAY:

FRIDAY:

SATURDAY:

SUNDAY:

ANSWERED PRAYERS & THINGS I'M THANKFUL FOR THIS WEEK:

MY PRAYER NOTES FOR THE WEEK OF _____ TO _____

MONDAY:

TUESDAY:

WEDNESDAY:

THURSDAY:

FRIDAY:

SATURDAY:

SUNDAY:

ANSWERED PRAYERS & THINGS I'M THANKFUL FOR THIS WEEK:

_____

_____

_____

_____

_____

_____

MY PRAYER NOTES FOR THE WEEK OF _____ TO _____

MONDAY:

_____
_____
_____
_____

TUESDAY:

_____
_____
_____
_____

WEDNESDAY:

_____
_____
_____
_____

THURSDAY:

_____
_____
_____
_____

FRiDAY:

SATURDAY:

SUNDAY:

ANSWERED PRAYERS & THiNGS i'M THANKFUL FOR THiS WEEK:

MY PRAYER NOTES FOR THE WEEK OF _____ TO _____

MONDAY:

TUESDAY:

WEDNESDAY:

THURSDAY:

FRIDAY:

SATURDAY:

SUNDAY:

ANSWERED PRAYERS & THINGS I'M THANKFUL FOR THIS WEEK:

_____

_____

_____

_____

_____

_____

MY PRAYER NOTES FOR THE WEEK OF _____ TO _____

MONDAY:

TUESDAY:

WEDNESDAY:

THURSDAY:

FRIDAY:

- -
- -
- -
- -

SATURDAY:

- -
- -
- -
- -

SUNDAY:

- -
- -
- -
- -

ANSWERED PRAYERS & THINGS I'M THANKFUL FOR THIS WEEK:

MY PRAYER NOTES FOR THE WEEK OF _____ TO _____

MONDAY:

TUESDAY:

WEDNESDAY:

THURSDAY:

FRIDAY:

SATURDAY:

SUNDAY:

ANSWERED PRAYERS & THINGS I'M THANKFUL FOR THIS WEEK:

MY PRAYER NOTES FOR THE WEEK OF _____ TO _____

MONDAY:

TUESDAY:

WEDNESDAY:

THURSDAY:

FRIDAY:

- -
- -
- -
- -

SATURDAY:

- -
- -
- -
- -

SUNDAY:

- -
- -
- -
- -

ANSWERED PRAYERS & THINGS I'M THANKFUL FOR THIS WEEK:

MY PRAYER NOTES FOR THE WEEK OF _____ TO _____

MONDAY:

TUESDAY:

WEDNESDAY:

THURSDAY:

FRIDAY:

SATURDAY:

SUNDAY:

ANSWERED PRAYERS & THINGS I'M THANKFUL FOR THIS WEEK:

MY PRAYER NOTES FOR THE WEEK OF _____ TO _____

MONDAY:

TUESDAY:

WEDNESDAY:

THURSDAY:

FRIDAY:

SATURDAY:

SUNDAY:

ANSWERED PRAYERS & THINGS I'M THANKFUL FOR THIS WEEK:

MY PRAYER NOTES FOR THE WEEK OF _____ TO _____

MONDAY:

TUESDAY:

WEDNESDAY:

THURSDAY:

FRiDAY:

SATURDAY:

SUNDAY:

ANSWERED PRAYERS & THiNGS i'M THANKFUL FOR THiS WEEK:

_____
_____
_____
_____
_____
_____

MY PRAYER NOTES FOR THE WEEK OF _____ TO _____

MONDAY:

TUESDAY:

WEDNESDAY:

THURSDAY:

FRiDAY:

....
....
....
....

SATURDAY:

....
....
....
....

SUNDAY:

....
....
....
....

ANSWERED PRAYERS & THiNGS i'M THANKFUL FOR THiS WEEK:

_____
_____
_____
_____
_____
_____

MY PRAYER NOTES FOR THE WEEK OF _____ TO _____

MONDAY:

TUESDAY:

WEDNESDAY:

THURSDAY:

FRiDAY:

_____
_____
_____
_____

SATURDAY:

_____
_____
_____
_____

SUNDAY:

_____
_____
_____
_____

ANSWERED PRAYERS & THiNGS i'M THANKFUL FOR THiS WEEK:

_____
_____
_____
_____
_____

MY PRAYER NOTES FOR THE WEEK OF _____ TO _____

MONDAY:

TUESDAY:

WEDNESDAY:

THURSDAY:

FRIDAY:

SATURDAY:

SUNDAY:

ANSWERED PRAYERS & THINGS I'M THANKFUL FOR THIS WEEK:

_____
_____
_____
_____
_____
_____

MY PRAYER NOTES FOR THE WEEK OF _____ TO _____

MONDAY:

TUESDAY:

WEDNESDAY:

THURSDAY:

FRiDAY:

SATURDAY:

SUNDAY:

ANSWERED PRAYERS & THiNGS i'M THANKFUL FOR THiS WEEK:

MY PRAYER NOTES FOR THE WEEK OF _____ TO _____

MONDAY:

TUESDAY:

WEDNESDAY:

THURSDAY:

FRiDAY:

SATURDAY:

SUNDAY:

ANSWERED PRAYERS & THiNGS i'M THANKFUL FOR THiS WEEK:

_____
_____
_____
_____
_____
_____

MY PRAYER NOTES FOR THE WEEK OF _____ TO _____

MONDAY:

TUESDAY:

WEDNESDAY:

THURSDAY:

FRIDAY:

SATURDAY:

SUNDAY:

ANSWERED PRAYERS & THINGS I'M THANKFUL FOR THIS WEEK:

_____
_____
_____
_____
_____

MY PRAYER NOTES FOR THE WEEK OF _____ TO _____

MONDAY:

TUESDAY:

WEDNESDAY:

THURSDAY:

FRIDAY:

SATURDAY:

SUNDAY:

ANSWERED PRAYERS & THINGS I'M THANKFUL FOR THIS WEEK:

MY PRAYER NOTES FOR THE WEEK OF _____ TO _____

MONDAY:

TUESDAY:

WEDNESDAY:

THURSDAY:

FRIDAY:

SATURDAY:

SUNDAY:

ANSWERED PRAYERS & THINGS I'M THANKFUL FOR THIS WEEK:

_____

_____

_____

_____

_____

MY PRAYER NOTES FOR THE WEEK OF _____ TO _____

MONDAY:

TUESDAY:

WEDNESDAY:

THURSDAY:

FRIDAY:

SATURDAY:

SUNDAY:

ANSWERED PRAYERS & THINGS I'M THANKFUL FOR THIS WEEK:

MY PRAYER NOTES FOR THE WEEK OF _____ TO _____

MONDAY:

TUESDAY:

WEDNESDAY:

THURSDAY:

FRIDAY:

_____
_____
_____
_____

SATURDAY:

_____
_____
_____
_____

SUNDAY:

_____
_____
_____
_____

ANSWERED PRAYERS & THINGS I'M THANKFUL FOR THIS WEEK:

_____
_____
_____
_____
_____
_____

MY PRAYER NOTES FOR THE WEEK OF _____ TO _____

MONDAY:

TUESDAY:

WEDNESDAY:

THURSDAY:

FRIDAY:

SATURDAY:

SUNDAY:

ANSWERED PRAYERS & THINGS I'M THANKFUL FOR THIS WEEK:

MY PRAYER NOTES FOR THE WEEK OF _____ TO _____

MONDAY:

TUESDAY:

WEDNESDAY:

THURSDAY:

FRIDAY:

SATURDAY:

SUNDAY:

ANSWERED PRAYERS & THINGS I'M THANKFUL FOR THIS WEEK:

Made in the USA
Coppell, TX
29 November 2021

66644602R00069